ARTICLES OF INTIMACY

ARTICLES OF INTIMACY

Advise for Better Sex

VICTORIA UPTON

Advise the Heart

Contents

ISBN: 979-8-8691-2178-3
EISBN: 979-8-8691-2179-0

NOTICE: We advocate for a vibrant and consensual sex life as a crucial aspect of a healthy relationship, built on mutual respect between partners of legal consenting age. Our endorsement extends to the practice of safe sex, incorporating the use of contraceptives, regular medical check-ups, or both. Additionally, we acknowledge and respect the privacy surrounding individual perspectives on what constitutes appropriate sexual practices, dating etiquette, and beliefs.
Our commitment lies in providing responsible, professional, and supportive guidance on dating and sexual matters. However, it's essential to recognize that this book serves as a reference and not a substitute for professional advice. For specific concerns related to your sexual, mental, emotional, medical, or other well-being, we strongly advise consulting a qualified professional.

Passionate Insights: 5 Expert Tips on Intimacy from Women Who Know

Exploring the intricacies of desire and passion, it becomes evident that men and women harbor distinct preferences, especially in what they perceive as "hot" or a "turn on," both within the confines of the bedroom and beyond. While men often associate heat with maneuvers between a woman's legs, the truth is that there's a vast terrain elsewhere on her body that requires attention before delving into more intimate realms.

Even if you've successfully undressed her and she can sense desire in your eyes, it takes more than that for her to fully let go and savor the experience as she wishes. Fear not, for the following tips and secrets, generously shared by real women eager to guide you in "helping her," promise to elevate your ability to bring her immense pleasure and set you apart from the men of her past. Allow these women to illuminate the common pitfalls men encounter and the aspects frequently overlooked, empowering you to truly ignite a fiery passion within her, leading to an explosion of ecstasy.

Finger-Lickin' Good:

Allison, a 24-year-old contributor, opens up about the often-neglected power of a woman's fingers. She laments that men tend to disregard this sensitive area, focusing more on upper arms and quickly moving on. Drawing from personal experience, Stacy shares a captivating encounter with an older gentleman who, unlike most, took the time to intimately kiss her fingers, sending shivers down her spine and enhancing her arousal significantly.

To replicate this sensual experience, the next time you find yourself on the verge of intimacy, seize her hand and embark on a journey of exploration. With deliberate and tender kisses, focus on the backs of her fingers, avoiding excess saliva. Gently run your lips across her index finger, paying attention to knuckles and webbed areas. Transition to the front of her fingers and palm, taking your time with each gesture. A subtle bite on the fleshy part of her palm can add an extra layer of intensity. As you progress, trace your kisses up her arm, delicately nibbling strategic points. The key is to be gentle, avoiding any marks that might linger.

As your attentiveness intensifies, her response is likely to manifest in heightened arousal – a wetness that mirrors her increasing breathlessness. Continue this exploration, taking the time to kiss and nibble various points on her arm, creating an intimate connection that goes beyond the obvious.

By allowing these insights to guide your actions, you can transcend the ordinary and embark on a sensual journey that not only heightens her pleasure but also establishes you as a partner attuned to her desires. Stay tuned for more revelations from real women eager to share their secrets on unlocking passionate experiences.

Embark on the Alluring Odyssey of Neck Kisses: A Symphony of Passion and Sensuality

In the realm of intimate connections, the often-neglected art of neck kisses emerges as a potent elixir, weaving tales of desire and longing long before the era of teenage vampire fascination. Unveiling the layers of this delicate dance, women have been silently craving attention to another sensual area of their body – the neck.

Jenny, a sage in matters of passion at 41, attests to the magnetic allure of neck kisses. Her plea echoes the sentiments of countless women who yearn for more substantial attention in a zone that often receives only fleeting caresses. The neck, draped in societal norms and concealed beneath layers of clothing, emerges as a sanctuary of vulnerability and heightened sensitivity, patiently waiting to be explored.

Sheila, a vivacious 21-year-old, passionately affirms the transformative effect of neck kisses. Initiating this enchanting journey requires finesse, a subtle transition from lip-kissing where tongue and saliva play a minimal role. The key maneuver involves the delicate act of gently but firmly grabbing her hair from behind, tilting her head back to expose the neck – a move that may already spark arousal and anticipation.

As the enchanting dance unfolds, the art of neck kissing involves embracing both sides, covering the entire neck with a symphony of kisses, licks, and nibbles. The experience should be a slow and gentle exploration, avoiding any excesses of roughness. Shawna emphasizes the significance of being attuned to her signals, as most women prefer not to bear visible marks on their necks, and the delicate balance between sensation and restraint is crucial.

The magic of neck kissing lies in the sensuality it evokes rather than explicit eroticism, creating an intense heat that resonates throughout her being. Experimenting with variations, such as going behind her and employing a "grab hair, tilt neck" maneuver, or kissing the back of her neck and gently blowing on the moistened area, amplifies the sensory experience and adds layers to the passionate encounter.

For those feeling audacious, a further escalation involves whispering into her ear with a touch of dirty talk, setting the stage for future intimate encounters. It's crucial to gauge her comfort level and refrain from pushing boundaries prematurely, allowing the connection to unfold organically and authentically.

Gentle Dominance Unveiled: The Art of Balancing Sensuality and Assertiveness

Transitioning beyond the ethereal realm of neck kisses, the intricate dance between being gentle and assertive takes center stage in awakening a woman's desires. Gently but firmly grabbing her hair becomes a potent catalyst, tapping into a woman's innate desire to be "taken" by a strong and confident partner.

This primal longing, rooted perhaps in ancestral times, finds affirmation in the voices of women themselves, who express a preference for feeling a sense of vulnerability, especially if they are physically or socially stronger. Popular phrases like "take me," "ravish me," and "sweep me off my feet" allude to the desire for the man to assume control, leading the dance of passion.

It's essential to clarify that being rough doesn't equate to causing physical harm. Instead, a subtle yet intentional roughness, when appropriately timed and aligned with other forms of arousal, can be a powerful turn-on. Initiating hair-pulling gently and incorporating a variety of gestures beyond the usual spanking and biting can deepen the connection, adding layers to the intricate tapestry of passion.

Experimentation becomes the heartbeat of this dance, exploring actions like lifting her effortlessly, guiding her legs around your waist, or leaning her against a smooth surface. The alternating rhythm between being a little rough and seamlessly transitioning into moments of sensitivity keeps her guessing and heightens the overall experience.

This delicate balance extends to various positions, from pushing her down toward the bed to grabbing her legs before penetration. The art lies in understanding her thresholds, gauging her reactions, and weaving together a narrative that is unpredictable yet harmonious, creating a narrative that unfolds organically.

In the intricate choreography of passion, the fusion of gentleness and assertiveness becomes a mesmerizing dance, ensuring that every movement is an invitation into a realm of shared ecstasy. As the journey unfolds, the unpredictability becomes a rare and cherished element, leaving her in eager anticipation of what each moment holds.

Stay tuned for more revelations, guiding you through the nuances of passion, intimacy, and connection. The journey has just begun, and the exploration of desires and the art of connection will continue to unfold in unexpected and captivating ways.

Embark on the Art of Appreciation: A Detailed Exploration of Her Derriere

Delve into the intricacies of being a connoisseur of her derriere, an art form that transcends conventional norms and misconceptions about what women find enticing in their bodies. Contrary to preconceived notions, women, even those who may not traditionally regard their buttocks as particularly sexy, relish the allure of attention lavished upon this often-overlooked region.

Initiate a profound journey into the world of sensual exploration, redirecting your focus to her buttocks. This exploration goes beyond the stereotypical attention it usually receives during intimate moments and invites you to set the stage for heightened passion and connection, even before the act of penetration.

Guide her to lay on her tummy, setting the stage for a sensual experience that begins with tender kisses on the back of her neck. Progress leisurely down her spine until reaching the focal point – her buttocks. The art involves a delicate balance of gentle biting, nibbling, and massaging, all while respecting her comfort and preferences.

The appreciation for her derriere extends beyond the bedroom, showcasing your ability to elevate the sensual experience. Playfully grabbing or slapping her buttocks can be a delightful surprise, adding an element of intrigue to your connection. However, it's essential to exercise discretion in public settings to avoid any potential discomfort.

Explore the nuances of embracing her derriere in various scenarios, weaving a tapestry of sensual experiences that transcend the boundaries of conventional intimacy. The subtle brush of your palm against the side of her outer thigh, coupled with a suggestive look, conveys an unspoken desire that adds an element of intrigue to your connection.

Pamper Her Feet: A Gateway to Profound Sensuous Bliss

Shift your focus to the often-underestimated yet intensely sensual realm of a woman's feet, drawing inspiration from the cinematic allure depicted in Pulp Fiction. Acknowledge the stress and tension borne by her feet, particularly if she spends extended hours standing or walking in heels.

Rekha, a sage at 24, attests to the transformative power of skilled foot touch, revealing that a well-executed foot massage can pave the way to greater intimacy. As you navigate down her body from face to lips, bypass the predictable path and surprise her with subtle attention to her lower extremities.

Explore her inner thighs, the back of her knees, and gently nibble on her calf muscles and Achilles tendon. Transition seamlessly to pampering her feet with a meticulous massage, starting with an overall indulgence. Squeeze her toes together gently, knead her Achilles tendon area and heel, and employ precise thumb movements across the sole of her foot.

The right blend of attention to her feet can evoke profound arousal, offering a gateway to a woman's sensuous pleasure. Elevate this practice beyond the confines of foreplay and prelude to intimacy by incorporating foot attention into everyday moments outside the bedroom.

Surprise her with a spontaneous foot massage while relaxing on the couch, showcasing your genuine interest in providing pleasure without ulterior motives. The reciprocation for your thoughtful gestures will unfold in delightful ways during subsequent intimate encounters.

In conclusion, remember this valuable lesson – kindle her desires even beyond the confines of the bedroom, and she will reciprocate with tantalizing rewards, enriching the tapestry of your shared pleasure. Young padawan, consider this the culmination of today's teachings, inviting you to embark on a journey of continual exploration and connection, fostering a deeper understanding of the intricacies of female sensuality.

2

Mastering Male Vitality: 5 Guidelines for Robust Erections

Addressing the common challenge of achieving and sustaining an erection is a prevalent concern, with its roots often entwined in the intricate dynamics of blood circulation within the sexual organs. Contrary to prevailing misconceptions, issues related to male sexual performance extend beyond the phallus itself. Difficulties in arousal or maintaining it during intimate encounters can serve as a harbinger of underlying systemic issues coursing throughout the entire body.

Experts assert that erectile dysfunction may function as an early warning signal of arterial damage, a consequence of excessive stress, an unhealthy diet, or the incipient stages of specific diseases. Thus, the initial recourse should involve casting aside ego or shyness and seeking the guidance of a physician. Identifying the root cause early on is paramount, and any consideration of resorting to the "pill-popping" solution should only transpire under the astute supervision of a medical professional.

After engaging in a comprehensive dialogue with a healthcare expert and eliminating major health concerns, individuals can embark on a journey to enhance their sexual well-being through thoughtful strategies.

Mind the Problems:

Given that erectile dysfunction frequently emanates from blood flow issues, it becomes imperative to hone in on the health of arteries, the conduits responsible for transporting blood to and from various organs, including the penis. However, mental well-being exerts a profound influence on these intricate physiological processes.

Stress emerges as a primary culprit, adversely impacting arteries by contributing to their hardening and concurrently diminishing overall sexual drive and performance. Recognizing the omnipresence of stress in our fast-paced lives, it becomes incumbent upon individuals to proactively manage stress levels.

One effective approach involves dedicating 5 to 10 minutes

before engaging in sexual activity to deliberate de-stressing. Find a private sanctuary, whether it entails retreating to the bathroom or a serene room, and immerse yourself in activities conducive to tranquility. Stress relief isn't merely physical; it's equally a mental endeavor, and a strategic focus on controlled breathing can be transformative.

Take slow, deliberate breaths, redirecting your attention from the labyrinth of your thoughts to the sanctity of your body. This mindfulness exercise enables you to be fully present with your breath, tracing its intricate journey from the nose to the lungs and back out. By redirecting your cognitive focus from mental stressors to the nuanced sensations within your body, you lay the foundation for relaxation, facilitating more efficient blood flow throughout the entirety of your being, including the intricacies of the male reproductive system.

Extend this practice beyond the realms of immediate pre-sexual activities by incorporating de-stressing moments throughout the day. Regular breaks, marked by the same deliberate breathing technique, not only contribute to the prospect of stronger and more sustained erections but also usher in a myriad of holistic health benefits. Commencing your day with this mindful exercise sets a positive and resilient tone, rendering you less susceptible to the deleterious impact of stress triggers. In essence, fostering a symbiotic connection between mind and body stands as a pivotal factor in the pursuit of optimal sexual health.

This holistic approach doesn't merely treat the symptom

but endeavors to address the underlying factors that contribute to the manifestation of erectile difficulties. As individuals embark on this journey towards enhanced sexual well-being, they embrace not just a transient fix but a sustained commitment to cultivating a healthier and more attuned lifestyle, nurturing both mental and physical vitality.

Strengthening the Core Components for Enhanced Vitality

Now that you've embarked on the journey of optimizing blood circulation to your crucial anatomical zones, it's imperative to fortify the major muscles intricately involved in this physiological process. This not only empowers these muscles to efficiently manage the augmented blood flow but also enhances their ability to contract and release with heightened vigor, ensuring a more robust pumping action for improved circulation.

Initiating a regimen of kegel exercises stands out as a stellar starting point. These exercises entail the deliberate contraction and release of muscles reminiscent of those employed when endeavoring to interrupt the flow of urine midstream. Alternatively, the tightening of your anus can also engage these pivotal muscles. For an optimum routine, amalgamate the simulated cessation of urine flow with the firm contraction of your anus. Constrict these muscles, sustain the contraction for up to 10 seconds, and then gently release, constituting a single repetition. Commence with a modest

5 repetitions daily, progressively advancing to approximately 20 repetitions.

These exercises exhibit versatility, accommodating various settings such as sitting in front of your computer or discreetly integrating them into your routine during a meeting. Alternatively, you can seamlessly incorporate these exercises while reclining in bed. A word of caution is warranted here – moderation is key, especially for those new to these exercises. Consistent practice with a smaller number of daily repetitions far outweighs the potential discomfort associated with an intensive yet infrequent workout.

Revitalizing Circulatory Vigor

Taking your commitment to circulatory health a step further involves incorporating regular cardio-style activities into your lifestyle. Whether it's cycling, jogging, or engaging in the invigorating rhythm of jumping jacks, these activities contribute significantly to an overall enhancement in blood circulation.

Commence this endeavor gradually, even if it means starting with a mere 5 minutes and progressively working your way up to a commendable 30 minutes per day. If necessary, consider an alternating schedule, such as engaging in this activity every other day. The inclusion of cardio into your lifestyle offers a dual advantage, not only promoting improved blood flow but also facilitating weight loss through heightened physical activity.

This dual-pronged benefit is particularly impactful, as shedding even a modest amount of excess body fat, especially around the waistline, can significantly amplify sexual health and performance. A reduction of as little as 5 pounds can yield positive effects on the strength and durability of erections. Consequently, viewing this aspect as a double whammy underscores its potential to contribute holistically to your overall well-being and vitality.

Elevate Your Nitric Power

Bodybuilders are well-acquainted with the significance of nitric oxide for enhancing performance. While many resort to nitric oxide pills for a performance boost, my focus here is on a different approach. Nitric oxide plays a crucial role in dilating blood vessels, facilitating increased blood flow, particularly to the penis.

The good news is that you don't need to rely on pills to boost nitric oxide levels; instead, you can naturally enhance its availability in your bloodstream. A proven method is to reduce free radicals in your body, achieved through a diet rich in antioxidants. Consuming antioxidant-packed foods is a safe and delightful way to increase nitric oxide levels, with dark berries such as blueberries being particularly beneficial. Incorporating these berries into your breakfast shake, smoothie, salad, or cereal is an easy and effective method.

Chocolate Reigns Supreme

Surprisingly, dark chocolate also boasts health benefits, including its ability to induce artery dilation—a parallel effect to that of dark berries. A modest intake of under 2 ounces per day of high-quality dark chocolate containing at least 70% cocoa is recommended. Whether enjoyed as a snack or post-meal treat, incorporating dark chocolate into your routine can contribute to improved arterial health.

While lighter chocolate versions with less than 70% cocoa can also offer benefits, a higher quantity may be required to achieve the desired effects. However, moderation is crucial to prevent overindulgence and potential weight gain.

Crucial Tips for Healthy Blood Flow

The shared advice emphasizes that healthy blood flow, particularly to sexual organs, is fundamental to achieving robust and enduring erections. By prioritizing arterial health and overall well-being, you can enhance the quality of your erections and sexual experiences.

Implementing the straightforward tips provided in this report is both simple and immediately actionable. Waiting until erectile issues become severe is discouraged, as erectile dysfunction can be an early indicator of more serious underlying problems or diseases. Regular health check-ups, coupled with the guidance offered, can lead to not only improved erectile function but also enhanced confidence in your inter-actions with women both inside and outside the bedroom.

Furthermore, don't be surprised if you discover additional health benefits stemming from the application of these techniques. Taking a proactive approach to your arterial health can yield positive outcomes that extend beyond the realm of sexual well-being.

3

Unlocking Bedroom Longevity: 5 Secrets for Lasting Power

Navigating the realm of sexual endurance often involves a diverse array of methods, encompassing techniques, exercises, devices, aids, and pharmaceutical interventions, all promising to extend one's performance. However, the crux of the matter, as many discover, lies not so much in the physical aspects but in the intricate landscape of the mind. Conditioning, cultivated over years or even decades, shapes the responses of many men, compelling them to reach climax swiftly. While comprehensive approaches to addressing premature ejaculation may require time and patience, there is an increasing interest in exploring instant solutions that yield immediate results.

The Perception of Sexual Duration

Unrealistic depictions of sexual encounters in romantic movies often set the stage for misplaced expectations. The dramatized portrayal of sex lasting the entire day or weekend may contribute to a sense of inadequacy for individuals striving to meet these cinematic fantasies. Contrary to these embellished narratives, the reality of a satisfactory sexual experience generally spans around 30 minutes, with variations. Acknowledging and embracing this realistic timeframe becomes pivotal in alleviating the undue performance pressure individuals may impose on themselves. While occasional extended adventures aligning with cinematic fantasies are undoubtedly enjoyable, it's crucial to recognize that most encounters need not surpass the 30-40 minute range.

Instant Solutions: A Pragmatic Approach

In the pursuit of immediate solutions for lasting longer in the bedroom, particularly for those averse to relying on pharmaceutical interventions, various approaches come to the forefront. One such approach involves letting the partner take charge, with certain sexual positions strategically minimizing direct penis stimulation. This, in turn, extends the performance time, offering a viable alternative for those seeking quick fixes. A notable position in this context is when the woman is on top, adopting a sitting or straddling posture. Optimal results are achieved when the man is lying down, reducing direct stimulation. Encouraging a slower pace during this position proves effective in managing friction and mitigating the risk of premature climax.

Beyond Physical Positions: Enhancing the Experience

Elevating the sexual experience involves considerations beyond mere physical positions. Introducing nuanced tactile sensations adds layers to the encounter, with actions like running palms along the partner's body or caressing specific areas contributing to a heightened sensory experience. Beyond diversifying the physical interactions, such engagement serves as a catalyst for the partner to let go and immerse themselves more fully in the encounter.

In conclusion, immediate strategies for lasting longer in the bedroom present a pragmatic and accessible alternative to more protracted solutions. By acknowledging realistic timeframes, experimenting with various techniques, and fostering an environment conducive to prolonged pleasure, individuals can pave the way for a more satisfying and enduring sexual experience.

Unveiling the Art of Prolonged Intimacy: A Holistic Exploration

In the intricate dance of human intimacy, the quest for enduring sexual stamina weaves through an intricate tapestry of techniques, exercises, devices, aids, and pharmaceutical interventions. While an extensive array of options adorns this tapestry, the psychological dimension emerges as a linchpin in the pursuit of lasting longer in the bedroom. Delving into the depths of this realm, the conditioning of one's body and mind takes center stage, with men inadvertently training themselves for swift climaxes. In the vast landscape of addressing premature ejaculation, a nuanced understanding is required, embracing both immediate solutions and holistic approaches that promise sustained results over time.

Unraveling the "Ladies First" Approach

The timeless adage "Ladies First" takes on profound significance in the context of prolonged intimacy. Positioned as an instant fix, this approach transcends the physical act, delving into the realms of psychology and connection. Beyond the conventional wisdom of prioritizing foreplay, the emphasis lies in creating an environment of unhurried exploration. By immersing oneself in the intricacies of her desires, navigating unpredictably through various erogenous zones, and introducing an element of surprise, the narrative shifts from performance anxiety to shared pleasure. This intentional focus not only alleviates pressure but fosters an environment where both partners can revel in the richness of the experience.

Navigating the Complex Terrain of Mental Focus

In the intricate interplay of the mind and body, mental focus emerges as a powerful determinant of the duration of intimate encounters. Departing from conventional advice that seeks to distract the mind, a paradigm shift encourages an immersion in the present moment. Acknowledging the profound impact of mental states on the climax, the recommendation is to transcend the fixation on orgasm. Instead, redirecting attention to the unfolding moments, shared pleasures, and the entirety of the sensual experience becomes the cornerstone. This shift not only prolongs the encounter but also expands the spectrum of pleasure sensations throughout the entire body.

Encore Performance: A Symphony of Connection

An additional facet in the repertoire of lasting longer is the concept of an "encore performance." Rather than viewing an early climax as a hurdle, this approach seamlessly transitions the focus back to the partner, making her pleasure the focal point. Creating a judgment-free space, devoid of performance pressure, ensures that both partners can relish the experience without unnecessary stress. Intriguingly, some individuals opt for a "planned execution" strategy, addressing premature ejaculation privately before engaging in partnered intimacy.

The Tapestry of Prolonged Intimacy: A Holistic Mosaic

In conclusion, the landscape of lasting longer in the bedroom emerges as a multifaceted mosaic, woven from diverse strategies that cater to immediate needs and enduring transformations. By navigating this intricate tapestry, individuals can not only prolong their intimate encounters but also foster a deeper, more profound connection with their partners. The art of prolonged intimacy, thus, extends beyond mere physicality, embracing the holistic nature of human connection and pleasure.

Mastering the Pinnacle: Elevating Intimacy through Proven Techniques

Embarking on the journey of enhancing one's intimate experiences is a pursuit that invites exploration, understanding, and the incorporation of strategic techniques. In our quest for prolonged satisfaction, let's delve even deeper into the art of pacing, employing additional methods that go beyond the conventional and empower individuals to master the nuances of intimacy.

Press the Pause Button: A Tactical Maneuver Unveiled

In the intricate dance of passion, the prospect of a premature climax can be a fleeting concern. Enter the "Press the Pause Button" technique—a quick, tactical maneuver designed to offer a brief reprieve. Should the impending explosion loom, a momentary pause coupled with gentle pressure just below the head of the penis becomes the key to a strategic delay. With a clamping motion using two fingers, one on top and one below, focused on the underside of the penis, this method temporarily restrains the influx of blood, affording the individual the opportunity to regain composure. As a versatile tool, it grants control over the rhythm of intimacy, ensuring the ability to resume activities and extend the experience.

Extend Your Finish Line: A Mindful Approach Unraveled

While not an instantaneous remedy, the "Extend Your Finish Line" technique emerges as a mindful strategy to retrain both body and mind for prolonged enjoyment. Acknowledging the prevailing mental conditioning that prompts a hastened climax during solo endeavors, the individual deliberately slows down, striving to elongate the experience by up to five additional minutes. Nearing climax, a graceful retreat, a short break, and calming deep breaths form a ritual that can be repeated up to three times. This practice, honed during solo sessions, seamlessly transitions into partnered encounters, providing moments of control and the potential to extend performance time by 10 to 15 minutes.

Embracing the Mental Shift: Beyond the Finish Line

Central to the journey towards prolonged satisfaction is the understanding that premature climax is a common occurrence for many individuals, irrespective of perceived prowess. Embracing this realization instigates a fundamental mental shift, significantly reducing the frequency of premature climaxes. Armed with instant and mindful techniques, individuals not only gain control over their performance but also foster a newfound confidence in navigating the intricate landscape of intimate connection. This ongoing exploration is fortified by these invaluable tools, serving as steadfast companions in the pursuit of enduring pleasure.

The Symphony of Sensuality: Orchestrating the Ultimate Connection

As we continue our odyssey in the realm of heightened intimacy, the tools presented here contribute to the symphony of sensuality. Each technique serves as a unique note, harmonizing with the others to create a melody that is personal, dynamic, and endlessly evolving. In the orchestra of pleasure, individuals find themselves not only as skilled performers but as maestros of their own unique symphony—a composition that resonates with enduring satisfaction and the artistry of profound connection.

4

Unveiling the Enigma: 5 Intimate Revelations Women Keep Close to Their Hearts

In the realm of intimate connections, there exists a subset of men who, regrettably, pay minimal attention to a woman's pleasure, emotions, and thoughts during the sacred act of lovemaking. If you find yourself invested in perusing this exclusive report, you've already distinguished yourself from the majority of men, signaling a commendable desire to delve deeper into understanding and, perhaps, enhancing your abilities.

The conventional male perspective on "sex secrets" often

revolves around techniques and maneuvers. The ceaseless quest for novel tricks that promise to elicit wild, exhilarating orgasms dominates the male narrative. However, women, being unique beings with distinct perspectives, harbor thoughts during intimate moments that extend beyond the confines of technique.

Unveiling the enigma of a woman's thoughts during sex can be challenging, given the intricacies of the female psyche. Women, in general, tend to keep their innermost desires and thoughts shrouded in secrecy, especially when it comes to matters of intimacy. Fear not, for I am here to impart insights into five clandestine musings and desires that women harbor about sex – revelations they seldom articulate but fervently wish you comprehended.

To embark on this enlightening journey, let's rewind to your first intimate encounter. Whether it was your initial foray into the world of physical intimacy or the maiden voyage with a new partner, recall the mix of nerves, anxiety, and self-conscious thoughts that permeated your mind. Similarly, women, more often than not, experience these sentiments, particularly when navigating uncharted waters with a new partner.

It's crucial to recognize that while some women exude confidence, comfort, and self-assuredness in matters of sexuality, a considerable portion grapples with insecurities, especially in the initial stages of a new relationship. If you aspire to lead her into the realm of extraordinary pleasure, positioning yourself as a contender for the title of her most memorable lover, redirecting your focus from acquiring new techniques to creating an environment of comfort becomes paramount.

Instead of fixating on intricate maneuvers, consider the profound impact of making her feel at ease. The objective is to alleviate her concerns, allowing her to relinquish the mental chatter that often plagues her thoughts. By fostering an atmosphere of relaxation, both physically and mentally, you pave the way for her to immerse herself in the pleasure of the moment.

Now, let's delve into the intricacies of what typically occupies a woman's mind during the dance of intimacy.

Delving further into the intricacies of the human experience, it becomes apparent that the paradox of beauty lies not only in its external manifestation but in the internal struggles with self-perception that persist even among those commonly heralded as epitomes of physical allure. The scrutiny individuals place upon themselves, regardless of societal adulation, underscores the universal nature of insecurities and self-consciousness.

My encounters with women possessing physiques that could rival or surpass the ideals perpetuated in fashion circles revealed a consistent theme of incongruity. Despite being revered as goddesses by the external world, these women clandestinely battled insecurities, fixating on seemingly trivial details. The asymmetry of ears or the alignment of a pinky finger became sources of self-consciousness, challenging the prevailing notion of external perfection.

Understanding this complex interplay between societal expectations and internal struggles is crucial when navigating the delicate terrain of intimacy. The acknowledgment that even the most visually flawless individuals grapple with self-doubt provides a compassionate lens through which to approach the intricacies of physical vulnerability.

As a partner, your role extends beyond mere appreciation of external beauty; it encompasses the art of alleviating internal conflicts that may hinder the full expression of intimacy. In the context of shared vulnerability, the act of disrobing becomes not only a physical unveiling but an unveiling of internal narratives, fears, and insecurities.

Verbal affirmation emerges as a powerful tool in this nuanced dance of connection. Uttering phrases like "Wow... you look... amazing..." or "Wow... you are... so beautiful..." assumes a significance beyond mere compliments. The intentional pauses interwoven within these expressions serve as deliberate punctuation marks, underscoring the sincerity and depth of your admiration.

Delivery becomes paramount in this orchestration of reassurance. Striking a delicate balance between genuine appreciation and authentic familiarity ensures that your words resonate authentically. Avoiding the pitfalls of sounding disingenuous or betraying a lack of intimacy with the female form is crucial to fostering an environment of trust and openness.

Crucially, the aftermath of such affirmations demands a nuanced approach. Dispelling the anticipation of a specific response prevents the imposition of expectations. Whether she acknowledges your compliment with a simple "thank you" or a warm smile, the key lies in seamlessly transitioning from the verbal affirmation to the next moment.

This practice assumes heightened significance when the woman in question deviates from conventional supermodel standards – a reality for the majority of women. Unaware of the gratitude most men harbor for the vulnerability she displays by undressing, women may succumb to self-consciousness. Thus, your role involves more than mere compliments; it entails affirming her significance and beauty, redirecting her focus from perceived flaws to the shared present moment.

In essence, your affirmations should convey the unequivocal message that, in that singular moment, she stands as the most significant and beautiful woman in your universe. This reassurance creates an environment where insecurities dissipate, allowing the authentic connection to flourish, transcending the physical into a realm of shared vulnerability and profound intimacy.

Navigating the intimate landscape requires an awareness that extends beyond the physical acts of pleasure. The intricacies of a woman's psyche during the act of lovemaking reveal a delicate dance between desire and insecurities that demand a partner's understanding and reassurance.

The multifaceted nature of a woman's thoughts during sex unveils a common thread of self-consciousness that transcends meticulous grooming rituals. Even with meticulous attention to personal care - encompassing showering, shaving, waxing, moisturizing, and deodorizing - many women find themselves ensnared in thoughts about the minutiae of their physical appearance. In the midst of passion, concerns about thorough shaving or dry skin can infiltrate the mind, sapping away the pleasure in an unwelcome manner.

A remedy for this resides not in meticulous scrutiny but in a deliberate demonstration of indifference to such concerns. Partners can elevate the experience by showcasing a genuine appreciation for the entirety of the woman, irrespective of perceived imperfections. Anticipating and refraining from any visible surprise or flinching at the discovery of birthmarks or scars contributes to an atmosphere of acceptance and comfort.

The aftermath of such moments demands a nuanced approach, wherein redirecting attention to parts of her body that evoke positive feelings becomes pivotal. Expressing admiration and arousal, with phrases like "You are turning me on sooo much," serves as a reaffirmation, steering her mind away from momentary concerns.

However, the complexities of a woman's self-consciousness

extend beyond external factors, infiltrating intimate spaces where scent and taste become focal points. Recognizing that women may harbor insecurities in these realms prompts partners to infuse reassurance seamlessly into the act itself. Uttering phrases like "You smell soo good..." or "You taste soooo good..." becomes a form of emotional support, delivered with minimal interruption to the ongoing pleasurable experience.

Transitioning from physical appearance to performance, the woman's mind may meander into uncertainties about her partner's enjoyment. Despite experience, self-conscious thoughts about adequacy and the satisfaction of the partner persist. The antidote to this concern lies in open communication and specificity. Expressing genuine enjoyment and providing specific feedback about actions amplifies confidence, ensuring that pleasurable behaviors are repeated and enhanced in the future.

In this symphony of shared pleasure, audible signals of satisfaction through moans and sighs find resonance. These subtle cues transcend words, reinforcing the partner's enjoyment and contributing to a reciprocal exchange of pleasure.

In essence, the art of fostering a mutually fulfilling sexual experience extends beyond physical prowess. It encompasses an acute understanding of a woman's intricate thoughts and emotions during intimacy, requiring partners to navigate the delicate balance between reassurance and passion, thereby creating a space where pleasure thrives unabated.

In navigating the intricate terrain of sexual exploration, fostering a woman's sense of liberation and encouraging the revelation of her deepest desires requires a delicate and nuanced approach. The dynamics of intimacy extend beyond mere physical interactions, intertwining with societal expectations, individual insecurities, and the quest for mutual pleasure.

Building upon the foundational concept of making a woman feel comfortable and confident, the endeavor to unlock new dimensions of passion unfolds as a refined art. Women often harbor unspoken desires to break free from societal constraints and embrace the unrestrained facets of their sexuality. However, these desires are frequently shrouded in layers of shyness, self-consciousness, or fear of judgment imposed by societal norms.

Empowering a woman to traverse uncharted territories in the bedroom involves creating an environment that transcends societal expectations. Partners are challenged to become adept in dismantling preconceived notions, fostering an atmosphere where she can shed inhibitions and embrace her primal instincts. The pursuit of uninhibited pleasure necessitates the cultivation of an environment that thrives on relaxation, desire, and acceptance.

Within the intricate web of societal expectations, particularly around female sexuality, a partner's role becomes instrumental in unraveling these complexities. Consistent affirmation of her attractiveness, scent, taste, and the impact

of her actions establishes a positive feedback loop, reinforcing her confidence and dismantling societal constraints. This
unwavering support serves as the catalyst for creating a space
where her deepest desires can emerge and flourish.

The art of attentiveness takes center stage in this journey,
requiring partners to be attuned to subtle hints or acciden-
tal revelations. Responding immediately and with genuine
excitement becomes a transformative force that paves the
way for her to gradually open up and explore new realms
of pleasure. Post-coital discussions, where partners express
admiration for specific moments of enjoyment, serve as a
roadmap for future encounters, fortifying her confidence and
encouraging the repetition of pleasurable actions.

Caution is warranted when contemplating the introduction of specific desires, particularly during initial encounters.
Pressuring or coercing a partner into unfamiliar territory
risks not only the immediate experience but also the potential
for future intimacy.

In the intricate tapestry of sexual exploration, the specter
of comparison emerges, with women often engaging in mental
juxtapositions during intimate moments. Partners are urged
to embrace a mindset of confidence and security, acknowledging that the woman has chosen the present moment with her
current partner for a reason. Free from judgments, compar-
isons, or self-consciousness, this mindset lays the foundation
for an experience that transcends physicality, evolving into a
profound connection between partners—a journey of shared

pleasure and exploration that extends beyond the boundaries of the ordinary.

5

∞

Whispers of Connection: Navigating the Playful Tapestry of Intimacy

Navigating the Playful Pathways of Intimacy: An In-Depth Exploration

Embarking on the journey of sparking intimate conversations requires finesse and strategic approaches. The aspiration to guide a woman's mind into the realm of naughty and dirty thoughts demands not just curiosity but a nuanced approach. In this extensive report, we'll delve into the nuances of five effective strategies, strategically navigating the pathways that lead to sensual and provocative territories.

1. Turning Up the Heat: A Gradual Temperature Adjustment

The common pitfall lies in the premature introduction of

sexual topics, a misstep that can leave women feeling uncomfortable or even offended. The metaphorical adjustment of temperature in her mind parallels the careful calibration of a room's ambiance. Abruptly increasing the heat would prompt discomfort; hence, the key is gradual escalation.

Guiding her thoughts from flirtation to sensuality demands a step-by-step approach. This ensures she doesn't feel overwhelmed, allowing her mind to adapt before delving into more explicit terrain. The subtle nature of this progression instills the belief that these thoughts originated within her, establishing a connection between you and her newfound fantasies.

2. The Art of Subtle Teasing: A Dance of Playful Intrigues

The power of subtle teasing lies in its ability to stimulate imagination without diving headfirst into explicit conversations. Hints and innuendos, delicately delivered, serve as a gateway to sensual and risqué realms. Subtle compliments, drenched in a mischievous undertone, create an atmosphere of anticipation and leave her intrigued.

By strategically incorporating teasing elements, you test the waters, ensuring the conversation aligns with her comfort level. This dance of playfulness allows for a careful exploration of boundaries, ensuring that the interaction remains enjoyable and respectful.

3. Shared Fantasy Exploration: Building Intimacy through Imagination

Intimacy thrives on shared experiences, even those existing in the realm of fantasy. Introduce topics that encourage collaborative exploration of romantic or sensual scenarios. By inviting her to share thoughts and desires, you deepen the connection while gaining insights into her preferences.

Framing the conversation as a joint venture in fantasy creates an environment where both participants can express desires openly. This shared exploration builds a bridge to more intimate discussions and strengthens the bond between you and her.

4. Eliciting Sensual Memories: Tapping into Pleasurable Experiences

Invoke sensory memories to steer conversations toward shared experiences that evoke sensuality or romance. Reminiscing about a particularly romantic date or a moment of passion subtly primes her mind to associate you with pleasure and desire.

By tapping into these memories, you establish a comfortable and familiar context for discussing more explicit thoughts. This technique allows for a seamless transition into the intimate realm without causing discomfort.

5. The Power of Imagination: Unleashing Creative Thinking

Encouraging her to unleash the power of imagination involves posing open-ended questions that prompt visualization of scenarios. By asking about secret fantasies or alluring qualities in a partner, you create a mental space where she can comfortably explore and share her deepest desires.

This approach builds a sense of intimacy and trust, fostering a connection that extends beyond the physical realm. The gentle guidance into the realm of fantasy allows for open expression, creating a space where both participants can explore desires freely.

In Summary: Crafting an Intimate Connection

In essence, unlocking a woman's naughty and dirty thoughts is an art that requires subtlety, shared exploration, and a gradual unveiling of sensuality. Mastering these techniques not only deepens the connection but opens doors to a more intimate and fulfilling dynamic.

Embarking on the Comfort Phase: A Strategic Prelude

Introducing naughty, dirty, and sexy topics demands finesse and a strategic approach, setting the stage for a seamless transition. The comfort phase involves a deliberate and cautious progression, ensuring organic and comfortable conversations. Let's delve into the subtleties of navigating this phase, unlocking playful banter and creating an atmosphere of ease.

1. Establishing a Casual Atmosphere: A Prelude to Playfulness

Commence the journey by creating a casual and non-intrusive atmosphere. Approach the initial moments as if engaging in conversation with a platonic friend, avoiding overt romantic agendas. Discussions on neutral subjects like weather or current events set the tone for a relaxed atmosphere.

Exuding an aura of ease and confidence is crucial, steering clear of desperation or neediness. Building a connection beyond immediate romantic intentions lays the groundwork for a comfortable exchange.

2. Incorporating Humor: The Gateway to Playful Banter

Infuse humor into the conversation to bridge the transition to playful banter. Light-hearted anecdotes and well-timed jokes elevate the mood, fostering a positive environment for more intimate discussions.

Integrating humor into the conversation creates a shared sense of enjoyment, contributing to the establishment of a connection based on laughter and positive engagement.

3. The Art of Quoting Others: Indirect Introduction of Steamy Topics

In the comfort phase, employ the art of quoting others to indirectly introduce provocative elements. Attribute bold statements to external sources—friends, neighbors, or fictional characters—to subtly bring steamy scenarios into the conversation.

Crafting a story involving quoted statements maintains a tactful tone, allowing her mind to engage with risqué content without feeling pressured or judged.

4. Gradual Story Unveiling: Sequencing Intrigue for Comfort

As the narrative unfolds, adopt a gradual approach to story unveiling. Share intriguing snippets without revealing all the details immediately. Gauge her reactions to ensure comfort and intrigue, allowing the progression to align with her comfort level.

Maintain an air of tactfulness and hesitation, reinforcing the idea that you're recounting an entertaining or peculiar incident involving someone else. This technique keeps the conversation engaging and plants the initial seed of sensuality in her mind.

In Summary: Strategic Comfort Building

The comfort phase serves as a crucial precursor to explicit subjects, blending casual conversation, humor, and strategic storytelling. Mastering this strategic approach positions you as a skilled conversationalist capable of navigating intimate discussions with finesse.

Leveraging Surroundings for Playful Conversations: Elevating Interaction

Playful interactions and engaging conversations thrive on leveraging surroundings. From introducing entertaining games to turning innocent remarks into flirty banter, these techniques contribute to a light and memorable atmosphere. Let's explore the art of elevating the fun factor by leveraging your surroundings.

1. The "Who Got Lucky?" Game: A Playful Dining Adventure

Imagine being in a cozy restaurant, sharing a meal, and introducing the "Who Got Lucky?" game. By casually observing other couples, you create a shared experience that actively involves her in playful banter.

Starting with a bold guess about an unlikely couple, you weave a humorous narrative, fostering a connection through shared secrets. The game adds an extra layer of entertainment, making your interaction unique and memorable.

2. Playful Misinterpretation: A Flirtatious Twist to Conversations

Inject mischievous fun by playfully misinterpreting her innocent questions. Transform ordinary inquiries into flirty banter, creating an atmosphere where humor takes center stage.

By turning the tables and humorously presenting her as the one with clandestine motives, you add a layer of flirtatious charm to the conversation. This dynamic exchange builds a connection based on shared humor and playful interactions.

3. Crafting a Unique Dynamic: Shared Secret Adventures

As playful elements seamlessly integrate into the

conversation, consider the unique dynamic you're cultivating. Beyond mere banter, you're creating a frame where the two of you share secret adventures and engage in mischievous interactions.

Explore these techniques, adapting them to the context of your conversation. Each playful moment contributes to the overall narrative, enhancing the connection and creating a more enjoyable experience. Weaving humor and flirtation into your interaction sets it apart as a memorable and unique experience.

UNLOCKING THE PLAYFUL CONNECTION: REVELING IN "CHICK FLICKS" BANTER

Embarking on a journey of playful banter and connection involves navigating shared secrets, humor, and a delicate balance of flirtation. Let's delve into the nuances of the "Chick Flicks" technique, exploring how you can playfully engage in conversations that resonate with both laughter and connection.

Initiating the Chick Flicks Discourse: A Playful Confession

Picture a casual setting—a coffee shop or a relaxed evening. Share a lighthearted secret or confession, admitting your secret enjoyment of "chick flicks" and romantic comedies. Whether as a jest or a genuine revelation, the key is to open the door to a discussion about romantic shows.

By doing so, you pave the way for a shared exchange of favorite movies, memorable scenes, and the subtle art of playful exploration.

Inviting Her Perspective: Navigating the Cinematic Realm of Romance

Having spotlighted romantic shows, transition smoothly into seeking her opinion. Inquiring about her favorite "chick flick" initiates a conversation that delves into personal preferences, connecting on a shared interest.

Seizing the opportunity to playfully tease, mention that you understand the allure of steamy scenes in these movies. Her response, whether denial or agreement, becomes a valuable thread to weave into ongoing banter.

Injecting Humor: Framing Playful Scenarios

Humor becomes a powerful ally in this playful interaction. Playfully suggest that, despite public denial, women secretly appreciate the sensuality portrayed in romantic movies. Frame it as a humorous observation, creating a comfortable space for her to either challenge or embrace the notion.

Should she agree, amplify the playfulness by endorsing the idea that these movies serve as a source of fantasy about the perfect romantic encounter. The light-hearted tone ensures the conversation remains enjoyable and engaging.

Strategically Switching Gears: Balancing Playfulness and Respect

Recognizing the importance of balance, intermittently shift the focus away from sexual nuances. Short breaks from explicit topics allow her mind to acclimate to the playful interaction, fostering an environment where comfort and enjoyment take center stage.

Seamlessly transition to other subjects, ensuring a dynamic conversation that isn't solely fixated on sexual themes. This approach prevents overwhelming her and reinforces the idea that your connection transcends the boundaries of just discussing intimate matters.

The Art of Vulnerability: A Rare Connection

In a rare moment of vulnerability, express that finding someone open and comfortable with such discussions isn't a common occurrence for you. This revelation positions her as a unique and cool individual, reinforcing the idea that she belongs to a select group of women who appreciate open and fun interactions.

Acknowledging her openness and cool demeanor strengthens the connection, as she perceives herself as someone who stands out from the crowd. This sense of distinction enhances her comfort level and reinforces the idea that you share a unique understanding.

Navigating the Next Steps: Gradual Progression and Awareness

Having laid the groundwork for a playful and engaging connection, you are now poised to guide the interaction in a direction of your choosing. The gradual progression, interspersed with moments of lightheartedness and vulnerability, sets the stage for further exploration.

As you consider the next steps, awareness and respect remain paramount, ensuring a continued enjoyable interaction. The delicate dance of playfulness, respect, and shared connection propels the interaction forward, creating a memorable and unique experience.

In essence, the art lies in the delicate dance of playfulness, respect, and shared connection. Continue to build on the mental frames you've set, and when the time is right, navigate the unfolding chapters with confidence and awareness.

Navigating the Depths of Connection: Continuing the Playful Journey

As the playful banter unfolds and the connection deepens, it's essential to maintain the momentum and steer the interaction toward new and exciting territories. The journey is a continuous exploration, marked by a delicate balance of intrigue, laughter, and respect.

Building on Playful Foundations: Expanding the Canvas

Having established a foundation of shared secrets, humor, and flirtation, it's time to expand the canvas of your interaction. Introduce new elements that align with your connection, whether it's exploring shared interests, delving into personal anecdotes, or even discovering mutual passions.

Consider the unique aspects of your dynamic and use them as threads to weave into the ongoing conversation. This expansion not only keeps the interaction fresh but also reinforces the idea that your connection is multi-faceted and ever-evolving.

The Art of Playful Challenges: Infusing Energy

Introduce playful challenges to infuse energy into the conversation. These challenges could range from guessing each other's preferences to playfully daring each other to share more personal stories. The element of challenge adds a layer of excitement, creating a dynamic exchange that keeps both participants engaged.

Be attuned to her responses and adjust the level of challenge accordingly. The goal is to foster an environment where playful banter intertwines with a sense of shared adventure.

Exploring Shared Dreams: Creating a Vision Together

Shift the conversation toward shared dreams and aspirations. By discussing future scenarios and shared goals, you create a vision together. This collaborative exploration allows both of you to express desires and expectations, fostering a deeper connection grounded in shared ambitions.

Encourage her to share her dreams and aspirations, and reciprocate by revealing your own. This exchange builds a sense of intimacy and shared purpose, solidifying the connection as it ventures into more profound realms.

Acknowledging Emotional Resonance: Connecting on a Deeper Level

As the interaction progresses, be attuned to moments of emotional resonance. These are instances where the conversation touches on deeper emotions, creating a more profound connection. Acknowledge these moments and express genuine interest in understanding her on a deeper level.

Sharing personal stories that evoke emotions or discussing topics that resonate with both of you contributes to a shared emotional experience. This acknowledgment enhances the sense of connection and intimacy.

The Gentle Art of Escalation: Reading Signals

As the rapport deepens, you may find opportunities to

gently escalate the level of intimacy. Pay attention to her signals and cues, gauging whether she's comfortable with a more explicit or romantic tone. Subtle shifts in body language, tone of voice, or the nature of her responses can provide valuable insights.

It's crucial to proceed with awareness and respect, ensuring that any escalation aligns with the comfort level established throughout the interaction. The art lies in reading the signals and adjusting the pace accordingly.

Seizing the Moment: Transitioning to a More Personal Realm

When the time feels right, consider transitioning to a more personal realm. This could involve sharing more intimate details about yourself, expressing deeper feelings, or discussing topics that require vulnerability. Seize the moment when the connection reaches a peak, and both participants feel a sense of openness.

This transition should feel natural and mutual, with both of you willingly delving into a more personal space. The key is to maintain the balance of playfulness and respect, ensuring that the interaction remains enjoyable for both.

The Unspoken Language: Embracing Non-Verbal Cues

In the realm of connection, non-verbal cues play a significant role. Pay attention to subtle gestures, eye contact, and body language. These unspoken signals often convey more than words can express. If you sense a mutual understanding through non-verbal cues, use them as a guide to navigate the next steps in your interaction.

Embracing non-verbal communication adds a layer of intimacy to the connection, creating a unique and profound exchange that goes beyond verbal expression.

Conclusion: A Playful Tapestry of Connection

In summary, the journey of playful banter and connection is akin to weaving a tapestry of shared experiences, laughter, and understanding. As you navigate the depths of connection, remember that the art lies in the delicate balance of playfulness, respect, and awareness.

Continue building on the foundations you've laid, exploring new avenues of connection, and embracing the nuances of shared experiences. The interaction is a dynamic exchange that evolves over time, creating a memorable and unique tapestry that reflects the depth of your connection.

Enjoy the playful journey, and may it lead to a rich and fulfilling connection with the object of your desire.

6

Unveiling Desires: A Guide to Awakening Passion in Your Sweetheart

Congratulations are in order! You've managed to land an incredible girl – she's not just cute, sexy, and sweet, but also caring, funny, and faithful. Plus, the best part is, she's into you. Your friends are probably green with envy, and it's likely that your success involves some effective attraction and seduction tips from our previous reports or, perhaps, it's just your natural charm at play. Either way, you're basking in the happiness of a flourishing relationship!

However, there's a slight hitch – your wonderful girl tends

to be on the "good" side in the bedroom. While you appreciate her virtuous qualities, you can't help but yearn for a bit more openness, a touch more adventure, and a dash of "bad" to spice things up. The desire is simple – to turn your "nice" girl a little naughty, allowing her to explore and indulge in those fantasies and desires that have been lingering in your mind.

It's a common sentiment; many wish to enhance their intimate experiences by encouraging their partners to embrace a more adventurous side. The good news? Transforming your "nice" girl into a naughty one is entirely possible. It's about creating an environment where she feels comfortable, connected, and willing to unveil her hidden desires.

Here's the thing – there might not be a "perfect" girl right out of the box. Sometimes, the potential for naughtiness is already there, waiting to be discovered. Other times, it just takes the right cues to make her feel at ease in expressing her true self. Whatever the scenario, you have the power to bridge the gap and turn your nice girl into the naughty partner you've been longing for.

In the following sections, I'll share invaluable advice and tips that can guide you through this exciting transformation. You'll discover effective strategies to accelerate the process, making it more seamless and enjoyable than you might have imagined. So, get ready to unlock the doors to a more adventurous and fulfilling intimacy with your special someone!

Indulging the Wolf Within: A Nuanced Approach to Intimacy

Men, by nature, are often driven by a single-minded focus. Once they set their sights on a desire, their vision becomes tunnel-like, unable to perceive beyond the immediate goal. This innate tendency is akin to hungry wolves relentlessly pursuing their prey, attacking the challenge repeatedly until a breakthrough is achieved or, unfortunately, a metaphorical bump on the head forces a temporary retreat.

Regrettably, some men return to the fray with the same headstrong approach, not having gleaned any insights from the previous encounter. The one-track mind prevails, persistently dictating their strategies. The analogy of the one-track mind is particularly evident when it comes to intimate desires and, more specifically, the pursuit of certain acts of intimacy.

Consider the scenario of men desiring oral sex from their partners. The conventional and often unsuccessful tactics involve a direct, repetitive appeal – asking, begging, pressuring, inducing guilt, resorting to tricks, or even attempting coercion. This method, as evident, seldom yields positive results. In fact, it risks instilling negative memories and emotions in the woman's mind, creating a counterproductive atmosphere for future intimate endeavors.

It is at this juncture that a different, more effective approach is warranted – one that navigates the delicate nuances of desire with subtlety and tact. Instead of confronting the issue head-on, a more strategic and, dare we say, "sneaky" approach is advisable.

Crucially, the key lies in making her believe that the desired action is entirely her idea, a decision that emanates from her sense of agency and autonomy. The objective is clear: no one wants to feel pressured, coerced, or manipulated into anything, especially matters of intimacy. Such tactics are more likely to push the individual further away.

Consider the analogy of a persistent salesman attempting to convince you to buy a product. The more forceful the pitch, the more likely you are to close up, put your guard up, and yearn for a swift end to the interaction. This holds true even if the product is of genuine interest to you. The aversion to pressure extends to our closest relationships, where we prefer autonomy in our decisions.

Surprisingly, the realm of intimacy operates on a similar principle. Everyone desires a sense of control over their decisions and life. Hence, understanding and respecting your partner's agency is crucial. With this in mind, let's explore some tried-and-tested strategies to gently encourage your partner to embrace a more adventurous side in the bedroom, steering clear of nagging, begging, or forceful approaches.

Reassess and Reset: A Modern Approach to Navigating Intimacy

In the realm of modern relationships, the dynamics of intimacy require a nuanced and considerate approach. If you find yourself in a situation where your desires may not align with your partner's comfort level, it's crucial to step back, reassess, and reset the narrative. The days of pursuing desires with a "hungry wolf" mentality are over; instead, a more empathetic and understanding approach is the need of the hour.

Step Back and Reflect

First and foremost, if you've been making requests, begging, pressuring, or worse, forcing your partner into activities they aren't open to or comfortable with, it's time to hit the pause button. Give your partner the space they need by refraining from bringing up the subject altogether. This isn't just about avoiding explicit discussions; it extends to your body language, facial expressions, and emotional responses.

For instance, if the subject revolves around specific intimate acts, like blowjobs, resist any temptation to joke about it, give strange looks, or display negative emotions if the topic arises. The key is to drop it completely and allow your partner's mind to cool off. This initial step is paramount in fostering a more respectful and understanding connection.

The Cool-Off Period: A Necessary Pause

But how long should you refrain from discussing the subject? A reasonable timeframe is until you've engaged in consensual sex with your partner at least five times since you first stopped talking about it. This could translate to approximately 21 to 30 days, depending on your situation. If you have a more frequent sexual relationship, adjusting the timeline to a minimum of two weeks is advisable.

During this cooling-off period, redirect your focus to pleasuring your partner by prioritizing the activities they enjoy during sex. This isn't about manipulation but rather about nurturing a positive and enjoyable atmosphere. If your partner questions your motives amid this shift in behavior, respond with sincerity and a smile, expressing a simple desire for their happiness.

A Genuine Shift in Approach

Should your partner inquire about the change in dynamics, resist the urge to revert to a demanding or pressuring stance. Instead, communicate a genuine intention by saying, "I just want you to be happy." This simple yet profound statement underscores your commitment to their well-being and comfort.

Acknowledge past mistakes if you've pressured your partner before, and offer a sincere apology. Emphasize that you no longer wish to create discomfort and express a genuine desire for their happiness and enjoyment during intimate moments. This sincerity is key to rebuilding trust and fostering a healthier connection.

Moving Forward: Tips and Techniques

After the cooling-off period, it's time to explore a more modern and considerate approach to intimacy. The following tips and techniques are designed to encourage a deeper connection without resorting to pressure or force:

1. Subtle Suggestion Over Explicit Requests

Rather than directly expressing desires, leverage the power of suggestion. Introduce the idea subtly, allowing your partner the freedom to process and contemplate it on their terms. This approach eliminates the pressure associated with explicit requests.

2. Shared Fantasy Exploration

Build a foundation for shared experiences by exploring romantic or sensual scenarios together. Encourage open communication about desires, fostering a collaborative environment where both partners feel comfortable expressing their preferences.

3. Eliciting Sensual Memories

Tap into sensory memories by reminiscing about shared experiences that evoke romantic or sensual feelings. By connecting emotionally through past experiences, you pave the way for a more intimate exploration of desires in a familiar and comfortable context.

4. The Power of Imagination

Engage your partner's creative thinking by posing open-ended questions that prompt them to visualize scenarios. Encourage them to express their desires freely, creating a mental space where exploration and sharing deepen the connection.

5. Gradual Story Unveiling

Adopt a gradual approach to storytelling, sharing intriguing snippets without divulging all the details immediately. This method allows your partner to acclimate gradually to the idea, ensuring that the progression aligns with their comfort level.

In essence, the key to modern intimacy lies in empathy, communication, and a sincere respect for your partner's boundaries. By navigating these nuances with finesse, you can build a connection that thrives on mutual understanding and shared desires.

A Gentle Approach to Intimacy: Navigating Modern Desires

Embarking on a journey of shared desires requires a modern understanding of intimacy and a nuanced approach that aligns with your partner's comfort level. It's essential to navigate this terrain with empathy and consideration, avoiding the pitfalls of pressuring or rushing into uncharted territories. The key lies in inviting her in gently, respecting the progression of her sexual adventure, and embracing a mindset that values connection over immediate leaps.

Gradual Progression: From Mailroom to Corner Office

In the modern landscape of sexual exploration, envision the process as a career trajectory—each stage a stepping stone towards a more adventurous and fulfilling intimacy. Attempting to propel her from the "missionary position" stage to the "anal sex" stage overnight is akin to trying to leap from a mailroom worker to the president of the company in a single bound. It's not just impractical; it's a recipe for discomfort and potential disconnection.

Consider the corporate ladder analogy: to become the president, one must navigate through various levels and positions, accumulating experiences and understanding the nuances of each role. Similarly, her sexual journey should involve a step-by-step progression, allowing her to explore new facets of intimacy at her own pace.

Understanding Her Current Position

Rather than fixating on the destination, take the time to understand where she currently stands in terms of her sexual adventure. It's crucial to delve into her mindset, exploring her comfort zones and desires. Modern intimacy requires an openness to communication and a genuine curiosity about your partner's preferences

By deciphering her current position, you gain insights into the starting point for building on her sense of sexual adventure. This initial understanding sets the stage for a connection that respects her boundaries while fostering an environment conducive to shared exploration.

Building Blocks of Desire

Once you've identified her current position, focus on the building blocks of desire. Modern intimacy thrives on the gradual construction of shared experiences, fantasies, and desires. Rather than attempting sudden and major leaps, introduce subtle suggestions that align with her current comfort level.

For example, if she expresses an interest in trying new things, explore scenarios that complement her existing adventurous spirit. This could involve shared fantasies, sensual memories, or imaginative conversations that gently push the boundaries without overwhelming her.

Empowering Her Decision-Making

A crucial aspect of a modern approach to intimacy is empowering her decision-making. Allow her to take an active role in the progression of sexual exploration. Instead of imposing desires, encourage open communication about what intrigues her and what she envisions for your shared experiences.

Pose open-ended questions that prompt her to visualize scenarios, express desires, and contribute to the collaborative creation of a more adventurous connection. By making her an active participant, you foster a sense of agency and control over her choices, reinforcing a modern approach that values consent and mutual satisfaction.

In essence, the journey towards shared desires involves a

contemporary mindset that prioritizes connection, communication, and a gradual exploration of intimacy. By embracing a gentle approach and respecting her current position, you lay the foundation for a more fulfilling and modern sexual adventure.

Unleashing Shared Desires: Modern Strategies for Fantasy Exploration

Dive into the realm of shared fantasies, where the mind becomes the canvas for more adventurous and naughty thoughts. Understanding her mental landscape is crucial, as most people embark on new experiences after envisioning them in their minds. The mind serves as the starting point for everything, and tapping into her fantasies is a gateway to unlocking new possibilities in your intimate connection.

The Mindful Prelude: Initiating Mental Exploration

To embark on this journey, start by delving into her mental space. It's essential to recognize that individuals are more likely to engage in actions they've imagined. The key lies in getting her to fantasize about adventurous scenarios, creating a foundation for potential exploration in the future. This process involves cultivating a mental landscape that fosters comfort and openness to naughty thoughts.

Timing is crucial, and the opportune moment to introduce these explorations is when she's already turned on or engaged in intimate activities. The heightened state of arousal makes the mind more receptive to daring and carefree thoughts, creating a conducive environment for shared fantasies.

The Art of Whispered Fantasies: Building Comfort Gradually

The technique involves whispering fantasies into her ear during intimate moments, gradually progressing from simpler scenarios to more daring imaginings. Begin with non-threatening fantasies, such as envisioning yourselves on a secluded beach in Hawaii at night. This approach initiates a sense of shared fantasy that encourages her to enjoy the imaginative journey with you.

As the encounter unfolds, progressively introduce more explicit scenarios, discussing different positions, the potential incorporation of sex toys, and exploring territories aligned with your desires. The objective is to gently open her mind to exciting possibilities and opportunities, creating a safe and comfortable space for her to indulge in these shared fantasies.

Safe Exploration: Bridging Fantasy and Reality

It's crucial to emphasize that she's not necessarily engaging in these activities in reality; rather, she's fantasizing about them during regular intimate moments. The distinction ensures a feeling of safety and comfort, allowing her naughtiness to emerge gradually into the real world.

This immersive experience can seamlessly transition into post-sex conversations where you both exchange more fantasies. Encourage her to share her wildest or "secret" desires without judgment, fostering an environment where openness and mutual understanding flourish.

In essence, the modern approach to fantasy exploration involves a delicate balance of timing, gradual progression, and a focus on cultivating a mental connection that paves the way for a more adventurous and fulfilling intimate dynamic.

Decoding Desires: Modern Strategies for Relationship Adventure

Embarking on an exploration of your partner's desires can be a thrilling journey. To add a contemporary touch to your approach, we delve into cinematic inspiration, moments of "permissible behavior," and the art of dressing up and role-playing.

Hollywood's Hidden Insights: Extracting Desire from Chick Flicks

If you've been avoiding "chick flicks," thinking they're not your cup of tea, you might be overlooking a treasure trove of insights into her desires. Classic women's favorites like Pretty Woman, 9 1/2 Weeks, and The Notebook provide not just entertainment but a glimpse into scenarios that turn your woman on. Engage in movie nights, inquire about her favorites, and observe her reactions. Pay attention to subtle cues — body language, shifts in breathing — to decipher what captivates her. Subtly expressing admiration for certain scenes can discreetly communicate your own desires, setting the stage for shared fantasies.

Shared Cinematic Fantasies: Whispering Desires into Reality

Cultivating shared fantasies involves whispering into her ear during intimate moments. Gradually progress from simpler scenarios to more daring imaginings, aligning with the pace of her comfort. Initiating this exploration when she's already turned on allows for a more open and carefree mindset. The objective is not to request actions but to guide her mind toward certain thoughts, fostering a sense of autonomy and choice in her desires.

Moments of Permissible Behavior: Unleashing Her Inner Seductress

Identifying moments of "permissible behavior" is a strategic move. Events like Halloween or themed parties provide opportunities for her to explore a more provocative side, often restrained by societal norms. Encourage her to dress as provocatively as she feels comfortable, emphasizing the fun and adventure in the process. The key is to create a safe and supportive environment, ensuring she embraces her sensuality without feeling pressured.

Dress Up and Role Play: Elevating Everyday Intimacy

Taking inspiration from romantic movies, dress-up and role-playing extend beyond special occasions. Introduce it into everyday life, surprising her with outfits inspired by characters from movies she enjoyed. Let her creativity take the lead, ensuring she feels a sense of ownership over her choices. This gradual progression allows her to adjust and feel comfortable at each stage, creating an exciting and evolving journey.

In conclusion, these strategies are not about abrupt transformations but about building layers progressively. Enjoy the evolving excitement as you decode desires together, nurturing a connection that grows more thrilling and naughty over time.